For Dad and Patti, in honor of their five- 🐖 anniversary.
A. P. S. & J. S.

The dogs are for Mom; the rest of the book is for Roy.
R. C.

Text copyright © 2003 by April Pulley Sayre and Jeff Sayre
Illustrations copyright © 2003 by Randy Cecil

First edition 2003

Library of Congress Cataloging-in-Publication Data

Sayre, April Pulley.
One is a snail, ten is a crab : a counting by feet book / April Pulley Sayre
and Jeff Sayre ; illustrated by Randy Cecil. —1st ed.
p.   cm.
ISBN 0-7636-1406-8
1. Counting—Juvenile literature. 2. Foot—Juvenile literature.
I. Title: One is a snail, ten is a crab. II. Sayre, Jeff, date. III. Cecil, Randy. IV. Title.
QA113.S367 2003   2001052494

2 4 6 8 10 9 7 5 3 1

Printed in China

This book was typeset in Maiandra.
The illustrations were done in oil on paper.

Candlewick Press
2067 Massachusetts Avenue
Cambridge, Massachusetts 02140

visit us at www.candlewick.com

One Is a Snail
Ten Is a Crab

A Counting by Feet Book

April Pulley Sayre and Jeff Sayre

illustrated by Randy Cecil

CANDLEWICK PRESS
CAMBRIDGE, MASSACHUSETTS

1 is a snail.

(This is a snail's foot.)

2 is a person.

3 is a person and a snail.

5 is a dog and a snail.

6 is an insect.

8

is a spider.

9 is a spider and a snail.

20 is two crabs.

30 is three crabs...

Or ten people and a crab.

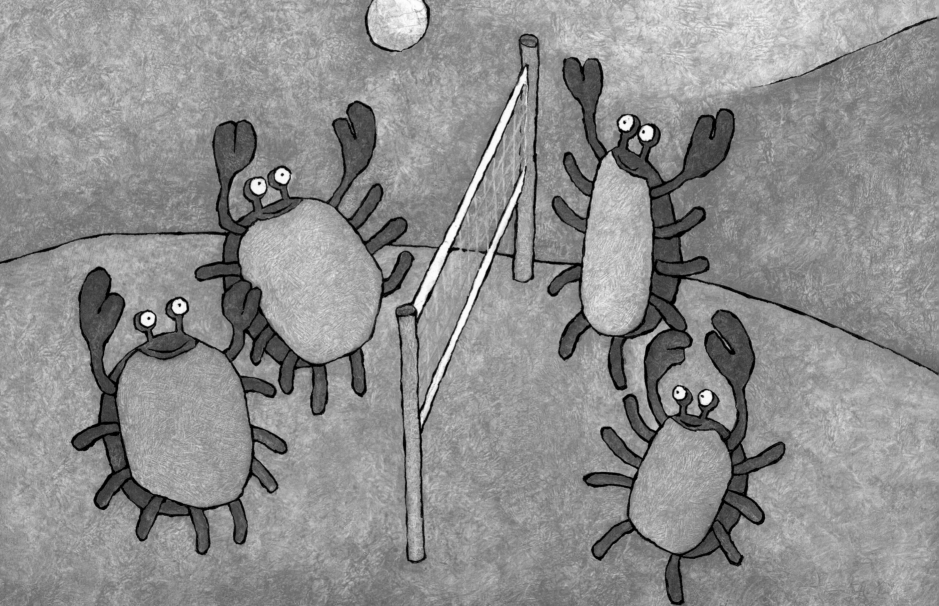

or ten dogs.

50 is five crabs...

Or ten dogs and a crab.

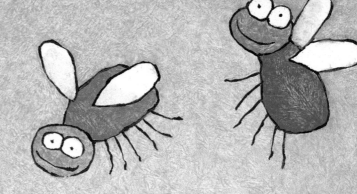

Or ten insects.

or ten insects and a crab.

80 is eight crabs...

or ten spiders.

90 is nine crabs...

or
ten spiders and a crab.

So,
100
is ten crabs...

Or, if you're really counting slowly...

one hundred snails!